洞月亮

CAVE MOON PRESS
YAKIMA 中 WASHINGTON

2017

Rules for Walking Out

by

Crysta Casey

洞月亮

CAVE MOON PRESS

YAKIMA 中 WASHINGTON

ISBN: 978-0692583197

Rules for Walking Out

Meeting Crysta Casey

I first crossed paths with Crysta Casey in the summer of 1979 at a two-week writing conference at UC Santa Cruz, to which we both had received scholarships. As a woman Marine at a writing conference on military furlough, Crysta created a certain buzz. She was pumping out the poems, working late into the night, fueled by the ever-present cigarette. I remember her dressed in a plaid shirt and slightly wrinkled jeans, as though she'd slept in them during these writing bouts. I also seem to recall a belt with a Western buckle. Or maybe I'm making up the buckle because she shot from the hip in her poetry. Her reading, at the student event at the close of the conference, unleashed a collective shot of adrenaline throughout the audience.

In fall of 2003, Crysta showed up in my Generating Poems class at The Richard Hugo House, a literary center in Seattle, Washington. The name "Crysta Casey" rang a faint bell; I had paused over it when I'd seen it in listings for local readings. I learned later that my name had also sounded familiar to Crysta, drawing her to my course listing in the Hugo House catalog. She had specifically stated in her scholarship letter that she wanted to study with Deborah Woodard.

During class introductions, I asked, "Were you at a writing conference in Santa Cruz 25 years ago?" "Yes, and let me tell you what happened *after* Santa Cruz."

Crysta told me and her new classmates how one of the visiting poets had advised her to stop being a journalist for the Marines. She was wasting her time, he said. She should be writing poetry instead. Crysta took this perhaps casually intended remark to heart. On her return to the base, she refused to report for duty, saying that she was at work—as a resident poet. Initially threatened with the brig, Crysta soon found herself dealing with its equivalent: a locked psych ward in San Diego. Possibly the only person in the history of the Marine Corps to go AWOL for poetry, Crysta was fond of mentioning in biographical notes that "she remained under the delusion that she was a poet."

Rules for Walking Out is the full account—finally brought together in one collection—of what Crysta saw and lived and who she met, for better and for worse, after she declared herself resident poet. It's about the minefield of class demarcations and sexual politics in the military and its adjoining worlds (in Crysta's case, in Seattle): the "rat-and-roach infested" Morrison Hotel, for example; some nondescript downtown city parks; and the Hurricane Cafe—a now-demolished refuge for outliers on the edge of Belltown. It's a series of dispatches, of searing vignettes of our prisoners of war, our own Disappeared, erased in institutions, routinely abused, and pushed to suicide. Crysta never made it overseas with the Marines, but she found plenty of material right here on U.S. soil. I have always felt that, when Crysta declined to serve as a journalist for the Marine hierarchy, she became the journalist—or, chronicler in verse—for her fellow Marines. She worked on their behalf, she appreciated and conveyed their essence and humanity (and gallows humor), and she was persistent. She had found her vocation. She already kept a journal, or daybook; she once told me that the daily entries helped her stay focused. (Crysta's journals and correspondence, now available to editors and historians, are housed in Special Collections at the University of Washington.)

Crysta devoted herself to *Rules for Walking Out*, developing and honing it over the years, and, in turn, *Rules* gave her purpose—in fact, it helped her stay alive. It's her core narrative, the story that she patiently told and retold. And it's the story that began immediately after that fateful writing conference in Santa Cruz. Creative writing teachers typically challenge budding poets to mine their deepest material, but I must say that the instructors outdid themselves with Crysta. I have the strong (if quixotic) sense that the folks who were at that long-ago conference need to know about Crysta, that they should be aware that their two-week wonder turned into a thirty-year sustained miracle. This book is the proof.

—Deborah Woodard
Seattle, Washington, January, 2017

Author's Statement

I would especially like to thank Sherry Reniker, my editor, and Deborah Woodard who helped with the arrangement and final editing. I am grateful to the following people who have helped at various stages or with particular poems: Wendy Battin, Nelson Bentley, Kathleen Fraser, Esther Helfgott, George Hitchcock, Heather McHugh, David Rigsbee, Janice Robinette and Robert Ward. Thanks to the U.C. Santa Cruz and Port Townsend Writers' Conferences for offering me scholarships and Richard Hugo House for the Hugo Prize. I am indebted to George Stamas, Monica Schley, Tom Angress and Libby and Landy Chapman for their emotional support. And thanks, of course, to the Veterans' Administration that not only supported me financially, but provided the therapists and doctors who kept me alive to write this.

—Crysta Casey (1952-2008)

For my Mother
and
Fellow Veterans

Table of Contents

Names have been changed
to protect the guilty
and the innocent.

Prologue

A Curse
—for Captain Bowman

You told them I was slitting
my wrists. But I had no scars
on my arms then.
You said, "In the bathroom
in her room . . ." The toilets
were down the hall.
You didn't even know
how enlisted people lived,
you in your officers' quarters.

I was a threat to you,
asked too many questions.
You wondered what I knew about
the Santa Margarita River Bridge
I'd discovered down by the hospital.
I did not know if it was built
upside down or right
side up; whether the water
was radioactive or drinkable;
if Central Intelligence blindfolded
people in the shed beside
it and interrogated them
until they told whatever
truth they knew . . .

I gave my name
rank and serial number,
said I was a poet. Beyond
that I refused to speak.

Sgt. Flanagan said you wanted me
dead. I wanted to throw coffee
in your face. I wanted you
to burn. The bars on the windows
repeated themselves, permanent
lines etched in my eyes.

I said, "I want to write poetry.
I'd rather pick up
cigarette butts than let you
use my mind."
You said, "I will see to it
that you sit in the brig or on a bench
in the mental institution
for the rest of your life."

Since then I've wanted to call
the police to send an ambulance
to your house in San Diego,
saying, "Captain Bowman is in
the bathroom slitting his wrists."

Prisoners of War
(At the V.A. Hospital, Seattle)

The V.A.

Saw Tom Lent in the Recreation Room.
He said, "When you paint me again
it'll be easier. They just took off
my other leg."

Divertimento No. 2 in D, K. 131 Mozart

The San Jose Symphony Orchestra is
practicing in the V.A. Hospital auditorium.
One old man wheels back
and forth in front of the stage,
no longer fighting his wheelchair.
It's a part of him
the way a violin is part of a violinist.
He's buckled in, his glasses held on
with cord.

A young man has come down
from the alky ward to listen,
USMC tattooed
on the muscle of his left arm.

"I'd like you to shorten the eighth
notes a bit," says the conductor.
A mechanical wheelchair zzzzs
across the wooden floor.
A blind man knocks his cane
against the leg of a chair.

"A dot above
the note," says the conductor.
The first violinist chuckles.
His belly rolls under his shirt.
The 2nd bass arrives late.
"Go on," says the conductor.
He taps the tall black stand,
"Staccato!"

"Resist the temptation
to ye yump!" yells the conductor.

zzzzzzzzzz goes an electric wheelchair.
"Before we break, I want to ask
the horns to come in very brassy."
The conductor stands on the stool,
his heels hooked over the lower rung.

Old men in striped robes lean forward
and the tattooed former Marine
conducts the air with a black ballpoint pen.

V.A. Smoke Shack

In a loosely-tied robe, the man with stump legs,
in a wheelchair, his gray hair pulled back
in a ponytail, swaps tales with another vet,
peanut butter in C-rats and M-16s
that clogged in the mud. One old man says,
"I don't know nothin 'bout Vietnam."
He's from WWII, lost on a long shot,
still betting the Kentucky Derby
that afternoon on TV. The nurse
on the night shift tells me about neighbors
who make too much noise getting drunk,
letting their kid jump on the floor.
"Shoulda never bought that place
near the airport. When planes take off
going north, the house rattles
and I wear earplugs."
The vets in the smoke shack
stare at the sky with lost eyes
when a plane flies over. A man says,
"They're going to remove half my face.
It was always my bad side." Another says
he has a cowboy hat like that other vet
from Idaho, but he doesn't wear it.
"I think I'm being punished," says the old
man who asks for a light.

Hell and Heaven

I.
In my hospital room, a boat
sails across water
in a painting on the wall.
White thermal blankets
ripple like waves
on the bed.

Dave has a photographic memory.
He can paint the pictures
in his head.
He asked the nurses
for his dandruff shampoo.
The instructions said to use
two tablespoons. He spread
it through his hair,
but the shampoo didn't lather,
so he used half the tube, rinsed.
Clumps of hair filled his hand.
They had given him his foot cream instead.
Now, he has several bald spots,
wears a baseball cap.

The vet named Freedom
limps with crutches.
He shot himself
in the chest and stomach
on the night of last month's full moon.
That was the day before he turned 50.
Now, he keeps writing the same letter
over again and sleeps a lot.

9

Today was another day of going up
and down between the 7th floor
and the 1st floor Smoke Shack.
Sometimes when we get on
the elevator, we press 7
when on 7, not moving
until we remember—press
1 when on 1, staying
put on the ground floor.

II.
In the Smoke Shack—
two men with throat cancer
on morphine drips.
Their machines go beep beep
when the battery's low.
Cowboy John, in a wheelchair,
is 23 years old. He severed
his vertebra in an automobile
accident. Now, he wears a hat
that reads, "I will walk out of here."

The man who had stomach cancer
is from Alaska and flies back
tomorrow. He's the skipper
of a fishing boat, keeps
flotation devices so his
crew's bodies can be found
in the freezing water.

Cowboy John is skinny.
He has 19 more radiation treatments.

He wears a smile, a light in his eyes
like a star on a cloudless night.

From the 7th Floor
you can see snow-capped mountains,
Mt. Rainier in the distance.
You can see white clouds
        puffed like waves—
7 in heaven.

The sailboat on my wall
is forever sailing.
If we are its crew,
we have fallen overboard,
our drowned bodies floating
in life jackets on the surface.

Paint by Numbers

I refuse to paint green or gold
across this canvas with miniature
puzzle-like spaces and blue numbers.
As if the colors could hide
the fear in my psychiatrist's face.
If I could paint a deer amidst
snow-capped mountains,
my psychiatrist's words would not
echo through the mountain peaks:
"Schizo-affective,"
he wrote on my chart.
"Suicidal ideation,"
he noted.

I turn the cardboard over
to my self-portrait, my frowning face,
sad as a baby's hunger.
I paint pink cheeks, red lips.
I refuse to try the clinic's bingo games.
I will not have a card that fills up.
I do not turn it in for a $5
canteen book. The hand that collects
bingo cards is warm, gentle. I wish
I could caress its lovely fingers.
Instead, I paint a hand
below my self-portrait. I paint
numbers on the fingernails,
mixing each one with purple hues.
They are eyes set adrift

in a sunset, casting silent embers
into a burning night
like a blacked-out bingo card.

Two Mirrors at the Bus Stop Near the Hurricane Cafe

The light's on. Still I can't see
the clock. I pick up the puzzle pieces
I dropped earlier,
a scene of maple trees.
I reacted badly to my new meds,
ran a fever. My head throbbed,
a jumping jack inside.
Now, I'm back to the old familiar
pills with the elbow twitches,
fingers counting nothing
or everything, tongue thrusting.
I don't care if I look crazy.
It bothers my doctors
and relatives more, strangers.

I wait at the bus stop
at Sixth and Bell,
not worried about the FBI—
they chase down anthrax
with no return address. . .

Today I start the new
program. Drug addicts
and alcoholics.

In the hospital
I didn't go through withdrawal.
My tox screen came out clean.
The doctors thought I was under
the delusion that I had used.

14

Maybe I wanted to experience
what it was like
to enter an alternate reality,
different from the voices
gossiping outside my window.
The voices make it hard
to put out a cigarette,
to turn off the stove.
I watch myself fall
asleep—to Oldies
turned low, a moment
of rest like a peaceful
death or regeneration.

When I walk to the bus
stop, I don't care if it rains.
I hold tight to
an umbrella
which works
if it's not too windy—
then everything turns
inside out.

I see my reflection in the window
of the bus shelter—it spins
into kaleidoscope colors
like the twirling yellow and red
maple leaves that fall
toward the sidewalk.

Green Cammie

One Week and A Wake-up to Go
(At Parris Island, Boot Camp)

I.
"Women Marines, lesbians, whores,"
Chaplain Birch says. We sit with our backs
straight as two-by-fours, hinged
to the wooden desks. Three months waiting
orders to Okinawa, South Korea, California
or wherever they send us but here.
"How many enlisted because of family?"
he asks. Four arms shoot above heads.

"Alright ladies, all possible pregnancies
up to the platform. Rest of you women
lean your heads back, open your mouths,
look at the sky. Okay you birds in a nest,
when you reach the corpsman, he'll squeeze
two drops of polio vaccine into your mouths,
while each arm is swabbed with alcohol.
The corpswaves will shoot one arm
with a shotgun of diphtheria,
the other tetanus. An X on the arm
for those who are allergic."

II.
"How many joined because love is a pain
in the ass?" the Drill Instructor asks.
Broom handles, with necks too thin
to screw in the holes of broom heads—
we build the necks up with a sock
someone lost in the wash

19

because its label fell off.
We sweep and wash the floor.
Our knees slop from tile to tile.
The remaining Wisk washes
the moth balls from our civilian clothes,
washes off black heel marks, polish, the print
of oxfords, our fingerprints from the walls.
Then we test our shampoo, concentrated green stuff,
use our fingernails like wire brushes.

Music sneaks beneath the door
of the D.I.'s hut. Our fingers
snap it up, as if we were on our knees
to pick each note from the floor.
Our hands grab mop sticks,
the gray hair slops down the back stairs.
We slow dance between the women waiting
for us to hang our mops upside down,
wondering if we can unlace
our shoes, and tiptoe sock-footed
across the wet floor, back
to our bunks.

III.
By now, we've learned to pad the outside corners
of our metal locker boxes, hope chests
and children's caskets, and
to drag them beneath our bunks
so they won't scrape.

Captain Bowman's Plastic Spoons

My combat boots sidestep
the mousetraps under his desk,
the electric cords attached
to the space heater and fan.

I dust around the letter opener,
the plastic model of a bayonet,
the gray intercom he growls through.
I dust between chess pieces
in the middle of a match—
the captain is an irate
world champion.

I dare to remove plastic soup spoons
from his coffee cups, where dried noodles
claw the sides like ivy.

I wash the mugs, flinging each spoon
into the trash, which I bag and toss
into the mouth of the Dewy Dumpster.

"Where are my spoons?" the captain yells
across the intercom, first thing
in the morning.

The garbage truck already chewed them.
My hand salutes the slimy bottom
of the empty dumpster.

The boot lieutenant chews his nails,
orders a detachment of lance corporals
to find some spoons.

Our fingers rummage through the paper
plates and cups from old parties,
when a spoon pops out at us
from the trash—

hinting at more to come.
I've never loved a plastic spoon so much.
In front of the captain's desk,
avoiding his mousetraps,
I snap to
and stare at the mugs
with their new plastic spoons.
The captain examines
the spoons with his fingers.
His mouth, an inflated pucker,
pouts, "Too thin!"

The boot lieutenant sends us
to the barracks for more spoons.
We find them in a box on the top
of the hot food vending machine.

Back in the office with the captain,
doors shut, my combat boots
sidestep the mouse traps
he has hastily kicked,

springing one. "My soup won't
taste good without the old kind,"
he grumbles. His fingers
reset the dusty cheese, then slide
down the handle of a spoon.

Running at Camp Pendleton

Look out when running.
Sticks can turn into rattlesnakes
slithering under boots.
Slow as I want—this is my attitude,
but it ain't true now,
I must run without stopping.
Hot water boils over my face.
Left side pinches, fist punches
below my ribs—breathing deeper.
The chest will stretch, stretch more.
Feet pound, toe, heel, up Mount Motherfucker,
heel, toe, going down. No curves, no glass,
no holes, close eyes, keep moving,
good except for my right big toe.
Fatigue creeps up on me like the captain
who is pounding behind, "Tired,
you're not tired!" The heart
in my big toe is ticking.
It grows into a giant black toe,
like a bomb.

San Luis Rey Officers Club

I bend my black low-cut dress
in front of the full-length mirror,
rehearsing the reach
for empty glasses.
No snags or seams run
the backs of my nylons. No black panties.
My skirt lifts like an eyelid. A hussy
when they look at me. I know
their eyes like marbles, flicking up and down.

His tongue sucks pimento from a green
olive. He draws a map.
"Past the San Luis Rey Gate, swing right.
First 7-Eleven, left. Do you dance?
Blue shingles. Nice legs.
White awning, a wooden
door with a knocker.
I'll leave the porch light on."

I picture untangling
his wash, his towel
looped twice around my bra strap.
My grandmother knew how to darn the holes
in men's socks, but I can only sew
the heel into a scar.

My name on a cocktail napkin,
the thin pages in his pocket
remind me of all the drinks

I've wiped up with these napkins—
my name shredded to lint
when he washes his jeans.

Adam and Eve

At Camp Pendleton, I drove
my 69 green Skylark to Lake O'Neil
and climbed a tree.
Below me, runners jogged
the track around the lake.
They couldn't see me.
I would smoke a joint
and eat my bologna sandwich.
I wrote code in a journal
I couldn't understand
twelve years later
and hid it from military superiors.

I showed my hideout
to one other person, Dave Miles.
Once, on a hot day during lunch,
we removed our boots
and waded into the water;
swam, cool, fresh, all wet
from shoulder to toe.
We had to go back to the office.
In the parking lot we ran
into McAdams, the driver
of our military van.
He happened to be returning
from the cleaners,
and exchanged two cammie tops
for our wet ones.
Our bottoms were still soaked.

McAdams liked to fish
while drinking Budweiser
in the hills next to Adam and Eve,
the two remaining buffalo.
Once, he almost slid the van
into the water
and it had to be towed.
McAdams died when
he tried to avoid hitting
a rabbit along the mail run.
Some say McAdams was drunk.
Pot was found.
There were bulletins warning
against Communists who sold pot.
The van flipped three times.
I went to my tree and cried.
McAdams had followed
the buffalo.

Rude Awakening in the Public Affairs Office

On Christmas morning the phone rang at six a.m. It took several rings to wake me. It was the Military Police. There had been a death in the San Onofre Area. They had no further details, but would keep me posted. I had slept quietly and unruffled in my uniform. I smoked a cigarette. I had dreamed of having Christmas with my family and hoped to be there by noon, eating Christmas dinner. The phone rang again. They had found a woman in her barracks room and they suspected murder. I phoned Captain Bowman. "Jesus," he said, "On Christmas morning." It was Suesette Bluing, a private. Someone was sent to find her after she failed to show up for mess duty at five. The suspected motive—she had gone out with a white man and the blacks were unhappy. By now the other phones were ringing off our desks— the civilian press, "Can you give us any more details on the Woman Marine?" We couldn't give her name until her mother was informed. They didn't know the cause, the fact that she had been knifed. They weren't aware that a tampax had been found inside of her. And I couldn't tell them—I would not be able to tell anyone until the news was officially released. I would go home with murder on my mind. Corporal Jan Burke relieved me. I was all packed, ready to go. I drove to the San Diego Airport in the car my mother had rented. My own car wouldn't have made it. I had a couple of drinks on the plane, though it was breakfast time. When I got home to Oakland, I was quiet around my family. We prayed for the little Lord Jesus, then opened our presents. I was given an electric typewriter and acrylic paints: red, yellow, blue, black and white.

Flying

The plates shattered onto the floor, all in a row. It was as if they'd been flung. Gunnery Sgt. Lopez looked sternly at PFC Miles. "They fell," Miles said. "Pvt. James, relieve Miles," Lopez said. "Miles to the scullery." Miles proceeded to break too many glasses down the garbage disposal. That was the last time Miles had to do mess duty. I had to stay on for a month, counting how much toast two Marine companies could eat for breakfast.

I had met Miles at Defense Information School; we studied journalism, smoked joints in the graveyard, danced on the graves of old soldiers. We were both transferred to Camp Pendleton for permanent duty. David Miles stood 5'9", had close-cropped blond hair and the stance of a Marine suited for Public Affairs. He hated to write. Trying to get a story out of him was like asking a two year old to go to bed without his blanket. He wanted to work in engineering, but they needed journalists.

Miles liked to build planes from popsicle sticks. He would fly them over the barracks' courtyard after rigging them with firecrackers. He built plane after plane and kept blowing them up. Miles wanted to leave the Marines. He had a skin rash that flared up with his nerves—he claimed that he couldn't work. They sent him to a shrink.

One day Miles disappeared into the locked psych ward. When I visited him, he was busy building planes. After Miles received a medical discharge from the Marine Corps, he stopped blowing up his toy planes and let them fly wherever they happened to go.

Self-portrait

In the painting, I'm sitting with legs spread against a chest of drawers. The platform on top serves as a barracks bed. I wear a camouflage shirt without insignia. Only black nylons cover my legs. A bathing suit bottom shows between them. My feet are partially covered by black, open-toed high heels. My eyes seem faraway, yet deep as a lake. There is a glitter of light on the lake, the sunset shining on water.

The officers wanted me to wear a cammie top and black nylons, a war belt, and high heels to serve them cocktails at the Officers Club. I needed the money. They tipped well. I only knew them as fellow Marines; I had my own male friend off-base. I didn't need them to stare at my legs, up and down, like an elevator with glass walls.

I felt sick. I turned the painting against the wall. Later the colonel came to inspect, asking to see it. I turned it back around. "You like to paint?" he asked. I took the painting to an off-base Marine. Someone searched my room while I was gone, leaving the drawers open. They wanted the portrait. I would give it back to them, what they had created. The painting faced the wall. The next day it disappeared.

Resident Poet

Captain Bowman had finally gotten to me. I forgot how to type. During lunch, I walked back to my barracks room, picked up my pen and wrote, "Resident Poet" on a piece of paper I hung as a sign on my door. The next day, Sgt. Adams knocked and asked me to report to work. I added, "I am at work" on the sign. The next day, the First Shirt knocked on my door. "We're going to take you to the brig if you don't come back to work," she said. "I am in the brig," I added to the sign. The next day, Lt. Davis came to my room and said, "We're going to put you on the psych ward." "I am on the psych ward," I wrote. "The truth is, I am."

The First Shirt and the Lt. took me to the infirmary. I was transferred in a government vehicle to the Navy Regional Medical Center in San Diego. I met John there—he was stuck at attention, standing straight, arms to the side, heels clicked together. There was no putting him at ease. I wondered if Ralph's flat head was a result of his jump from the barracks roof. He was there for possible brain damage. Anne refused to take her medicine. She was hogtied to a stretcher and put in the "box," a seclusion room. After standing in line, I swallowed my pills.

Two weeks later, I was transferred to Oaknoll in a medevac Red Cross plane. My family lived in Oakland. I called my sister. She said that Mother had been taken to the hospital on the same day. Her cancer was worse. I had forgotten about my mother. I requested emergency passes and visited her, busing from my hospital to hers. She recognized me, but didn't know if it was day or night, or whether or not to eat. "Do you know who you are?" she asked. "Yes, I know who I am," I said.

Green Cammie

Bought for less than a quarter
at a garage sale. The dead
remains left to relatives
who pack up. The shirt was like the cammie
I used to wear, costing far more;
a twisting of my body—trigger happy
fingers and targets full of holes
close to my heart, legs spread
open to officers who kiss and cuss
and drink too much and drive me
into woods where they keep
toilet paper in the glove compartments
of their jeeps for moments after
they unbutton my shirt and ask me to suck
them like a cherry popsicle, only hot
as corn on the cob. When I finally refuse,
they give me to doctors who order me
to swallow pills to forget, pills that slow me down,
make me so depressed I burn myself,
tattoos of shame. One day,
I stop taking the pills. I feel something
alive and churning inside that unfolds.
Now, I wear my green cammie shirt
as a jacket every day,
pockets for a wallet, keys and extra
cigarettes, the shirt stripped of name tag
and rank. I am the Private/General
of my own Army.

Boarded Up

If You Shatter Too Many Glass Houses, Your Own Windows Will Be Boarded Up

Mother, I heard you entered
the cancer ward the same afternoon
aides drove me via ambulance
to the Navy Regional Medical Center,
San Diego. I talked to the crazy
photographer whose body imitated
my every gesture, capturing me
without his camera, the musician
who sang to the chaplain, the M.P.
who threatened to shoot herself
and everybody else. We all swallowed
our psychotropic pills (except Anne
who they tackled and shot).

The doctors kept asking me,
"Who are you?" I gave my name,
rank and service number and added,
"I am a poet." But my poems
were locked in my locker
back at the barracks. I was afraid
the First Shirt would confiscate them.
I began writing furiously in a new notebook.

Glass Houses

1. San Diego: 3rd Floor Psychotic Ward

Could be locked up here three weeks;
the seagulls,
philosophers and cartoonists
of every duty station
dumped in one ward.
Last match,
smoker's cough; no phone call,
just waiting. I would rather have gone
directly to jail, sat out
two rolls of the dice
on a bench.

Monopoly doesn't put a space
on the board
for psych wards. The Catholic Church
disappears
into ancient order.
Black sheep, white artists and poets,
moon-struck herders;
alphabets of stars.

I threw too many
baseballs through the neighbor's windows,
firecrackers under empty dog food cans,
coke bottles,
fuses clear round the house,
well camouflaged.

*

*

Prison walls, the length and width
of a ship
in the middle of the ocean,
in the middle of San Diego.
In the galley, a washer, dryer, coffee maker,
metal shelf.
Fountain in the courtyard, birds
of paradise. The sun shines somewhere;
a shadow of stairs, steps
to the outside hall;
adobe. What are they doing?

I forget this woman's name.
I try to explain to her how
a drawer is solid
opening and closing
like people sometimes;
forks and knives inside,
wash rags, place mats, napkins
and pillow cases—
wonder when they'll let me go.

This is home for a while,
curtains on the barred windows,
old building; pipes and vents;
people with a leg on each side
of an earthquake fault,
cracked, pulled apart.
There's even a piano, a large
antenna on the roof, tower light
to keep planes from landing
too soon, the roar
of runway.

James talks, says his name,
how tall he is, 5'4".
He knows
some kind of code,
to get inside,
to name the feelings,
so muscles won't jerk
on their own.

Frank makes angels
flat on his back
on the dayroom floor,
wings flapping, tongue flung
against the roof of his mouth
neck cords tight as tent rope
afraid the halves,
pajamas, bowels, cries
will collapse
if he unties the note
in his throat.

*
*

Sunny day, down
in the courtyard
on mowed grass
near the fountain.
Barefoot, baggy
pajamas snapped
on the tightest snaps,
still falling down.

Navy blue
corduroy robe,

40

two big buttons,
three pockets.
We're not allowed
to wear our own clothes
even outside.

Squeak of technicians'
shoes. Frozen chicken
legs still connected to thighs
in the barbecue. Already ate
our potato salad, apple pie,
early dessert.
The sherbet melts;
the chicken thaws.

         *

         *

Birds on tree tops,
U. S. flag and two blue stars
on white, an admiral inside
on a cushioned chair.
I'm sitting at the head
of my bed, feet propped
on the window sill.
A guinea pig again,
the doctor can make me swallow
anything.

         *

         *

"I'm not hungry."
"Dinner's here."
"I'm not doing anything,
why eat?"

My clothes are in a pillow—
case, locked in a closet.
A fat nurse waddles past.
Flushed cheeks, eyes
of a caged parakeet.
Music on the radio.
My ear rings on its own.
At night, sometimes I think.

2. Taking Meds on Time

"You can check out any time you like,
but you can never leave."
                    —The Eagles, "Hotel California"

Anne takes her watch apart.
She explains how motion moves
from the wheels to the hands,
the minutes to hours.
"As the mainspring
uncoils, the detaining catch
releases one tooth
of the escape wheel

at a time." Anne's job
was to fix Marine Corps clocks,
the kind on school walls.
Then she began to remove their hands.
Anne has till 9:15 to swallow
the green medicine.
I already swallowed mine.
Anne is sure I'll die.

She removes the hands
of her watch. "They cover
the minutes like eyes
which shouldn't be blind,"
she says. Four Navy nurses

push through the door.
Anne throws watch wheels

like miniature saucers.
It must be 9:15. A stretcher waits
in the hall. They hog-tie her
ankles to her wrists
behind her back.

When Anne gets out
of the box, she tells me,
"I listened to my heart
marking time in one place,
counted the days
by the bruises I got
from the shot in my ass
each morning."

3. Navy Regional Medical Center, Fifth Floor

The day room is still.
Games, National Geographics
from the fifties,
ninety-eight pieces
of a puzzle called Tranquility,
two pieces missing.

On a shelf in the corner,
I make a game, stack white,
blue, and red poker chips
into a tower, knock it down
with dice, then pile
the chips again.
I load the bed
of a plastic pick-up
with pieces of the game Clue:
the noose, the candlestick,
Colonel Mustard and Mrs. Peacock.
When I try to drive,
the truck wheels are glued on,
so we park on the radiator,
till I feel the tired lines sagging
beneath my eyes.

Stretched on the couch,
face down in the rectangle
of folded arms, I remember
the night I woke at two a.m.
in the transient room
and air hissed through ventilators.
All is well, I thought.

45

Maybe not, caught between my teeth
like a thread.

I had posed in my friend
Sergeant Sanchez's room
until he ran out
of film. Now I imagine him being
murdered with an ax
over and over.
I wonder who developed his negatives,
if they were boxed with the rest
of his stuff, the evidence
of what he was. I was told his possessions
were all tangled with his blood, that I knew
the two lance corporals who left
their drunken fingerprints on his skin.
I don't remember their faces.

When I lift my head, the ping pong
table seems to straighten its edges.
Tiles of the day room stop tilting.
I'm still in one spot on the couch,
but the questions thread
through my ears, piercing
like my first earrings.

4. Visiting Mother

After three weeks, they medevacked me
to NRMC Oakland. Mother, I'm trying
so hard to keep up with my surroundings;
the next cigarette, I've forgotten you.

"You must eat," I say cutting
your veal into small bites.
"Put the plate here," you say, pointing
to a mountain of belly
under the white sheet.
"There must be a blockage
somewhere, to make such a mound."

The fork shakes in your hand.
"You'll spill it!" I caution.
You fork another bite, steering it
toward your mouth.
You swallow, then choke.

"It's not a bubble. I always said
it was just a bubble, the kind you blow
when you're a kid. It's more than that,"
you choke. "It's so hard
to eat breakfast."

"It's dinner," I remind you. "It's dark out."
I open the curtains. "It's not today anymore."
"Do you think my hair would look good
cut like yours?" you ask, dropping
your fork to the plate.

47

I notice your comb full of hair
on the bedside table. "There isn't enough,"
I answer.
You chuckle. "Maybe parted
in the middle or combed back."
You finger the thin strands.
Like Dad's, to cover the bald spot, I think.

"Here's another hair, if I'm not imagining it.
Last night, I had a nightmare.
I lost it all." Your fingers pluck at the hair,
finally brush it from the sheet.

5. Shifting

You want me
to find you
a new position.
I pull the sheet
and blankets down
your skinny white legs.
My hands lift your hip bones
to the sinking low point,
the center,
from headboard
to footboard,
a straight line
of bone,
skull to
numb toes.

6. Fences

There are rules for walking out.
Rules for eating in the dining room
instead of on the ward.
At first, you go with a buddy,
an elevator ride, then down a line.
There's a choice between
stewed tomatoes and string beans.
I can't make up my mind.

Frank sits at the table.
His roast beef finished,
he pulls out a finger puppet
made from paper. The puppet smiles,
is introduced as Arnold.
Frank puts Arnold back in his pocket.
When we go upstairs, Frank
and Arnold both quit talking.

Mark isn't allowed to go
with us yet. He eats on the ward.
In between bites, he wanders
towards the door. "Mark,"
the nurse calls.

"Are you a wanderer too?"
the doctor asks me. I don't answer,
but run barefoot ten times
around the cement rectangular
sundeck, ducking umbrellas.

The fence is bent
inwards. It's difficult to climb out,
but Mark pokes his toes into the fence,
scales the barbed wire.

He flies over the side, four stories.
They find him on his back
asking, "Am I dead yet? Am I alive?"

7. And in the end, Mother,

I rode the bus six times
from my bed to yours,
until they had folded
the sheet corners
without you.

Snow

The Boat

Kim came over the night
I found out I had a shadow
on my stomach.
She was a cross-dresser—
a bomber pilot in Vietnam,
now in my Women's
Straight and Sober Group.
We drank wine that night.
She told me she had been
the son of the president of Chrysler
in Detroit, and when
the song played, "I was not
the chosen one . . ." she said,
"I was the chosen one."

Kim lived at the Morrison Hotel,
a rundown, rat-and-roach infested
example of public housing in Seattle,
across from the Court House.
She lay in bed and watched T.V.
most of the time. Once she brought
a noose to the group, said she wanted
to go on the long sleep. That night
we talked, she said, "You don't have
stomach cancer."

I wanted to paint
a boat down by the water.
It was in a state of decay

but I wanted to capture the beauty of its shadow
on the water—like an x-ray.
I needed to look at the boat in detail,
the cabin doors, the life boat,
the flags flying.

Kim gave me her paints.
They did an M.R.I., shot me
with intravenous iodine. Still something there,
so they sent a camera down my stomach,
said it was fine.
Kim called to go out to Ivar's.
She would treat me. My answering machine
took the message. I never got back
to her. She hung herself on a Friday.
Two weeks later, I went down to paint the boat.
It was gone.

War

That Marine
serving in Iraq
won't have to
wash her face
this morning.

Jim

Jim is a Vietnam Vet. He watches television
and sleeps all day. He eats sporadically.
He doesn't get out much, but one day decided to go
downtown to the V.A. Regional Office
and make sure he was going to get an American flag
on his coffin. The clerk took down his name
and service #. He came back and said,
"I'm sorry sir, but according to our records
you're already dead."

Rain

I took a break,
stood by the fountain
near the cafeteria.
A boy about five
came out to the edge
of the garden
where water dripped
from an overhang
to put his hands
in the rain,
rub them together.
He stuck his tennis shoe out,
leaned his chest,
then shoulder
into the drip,
pulled his sweatshirt
open at the neck, said,
"Yikes! That tickles."
Put his hair
under, said, "Yow!
I just got shot in the head."

Poem for an Unknown Soldier

The flag at the park hangs
half mast. I asked a young mother
pushing a child on a swing,
"who died?"
"Orville Redenbacher did,
but I don't think they'd fly a flag
for a popcorn man."
I spoke with another mother
in the parking lot,
"Maybe it was
for the elections yesterday?"
she said, "That could depress
some people, but I don't think
they'd lower the flag.
Somebody famous or local?"
I listened to the radio, waiting
for the news.

The Sane and the Insane

My thoughts are more exciting
when I'm not on meds.
On medication, I think
of vacuuming the carpet
to get rid of any bugs
Bonnie may have left
when she curled into a fetal position
on the rug last Sunday.

At three a.m., she lit
three cigarettes at the same time,
put them in the ashtray
and watched them burn,
said, "Kaw, globble,"
so I called 911. The medics were nice
when they took her to the hospital.
She put on her boots
without socks, did not lace them—

I had to give a poetry reading
the next night. "Don't rock,"
I reminded myself, "that's a dead giveaway."
I think it was Robert Graves who wrote
in The White Goddess, "The difference
between the insane and poets,
is that poets write it down."

His Self-Portrait

A self-portrait hangs
above him as he sleeps
restlessly on the mattress.
His legs kick like a horse's
pawing the dirt, clump, clump.
In the portrait, his face glows orange,
the background purple,
the complimentary colors
of a sunset in Vietnam.
But the eyes, the eyes
(and the heart he painted
black below the left breast),
suffer the sorrow
of a drafted man
who didn't want to kill
and later met the refugees,
strung electric wire
for the relatives of those
he bombed. His legs run away
with his dreams, tangled
in the blue quilt of night.

I woke once to my husband
bare ass naked on all fours,
pawing the wooden floor
with his bowie knife.
I called him
out of sleep as he fought
the dreamed enemy,
and later, fully awake,

he walked into the woods
with a bottle of whiskey
and all his pills.
After three months, a father
and his son were looking
for fossils and found his bones.

My lover's eyes
are closed tonight
beneath blankets,
and though he is not at peace,
I will let him sleep.

Snow

It falls so quietly, I do not know it
falls, the off-white curtains closed.
I doze for an hour and a half,
all I have slept in three days.
Streetlights on the snow
whiten the night. I dream of men
hanging for the crime
of being, a crime they didn't mean
to commit, or was that a song
I heard on the radio? The snow
whitens their dark tongues,
their eyes open as though they will
never close again.

Afterwords

Crysta Casey

I first met Crysta Casey on the front porch of Richard Hugo House, where she often sat smoking cigarettes. That was a few years before Seattle's 2005 smoking ban required people to light up twenty-five feet from building entrances. That law may have seemed like a coup for public health, but it had some cultural side effects. Instead of drawing people from the margins into the warmth of the collective hearth, we asked them to stand in the rain in shame with their soggy cigarettes. We banished all smokers, even the ones who used cigarettes to feel a sense of containment, or those who used cigarettes to decompress, or to mitigate the effects of psychotic symptoms.

Our assumption was that lack of exposure to smoking would save our lives. But what human connections did we lose in that bargain? If I hadn't worked at Hugo House, for example, and hadn't encountered Crysta Casey smoking on the front porch each morning or afternoon, I might have missed my way here: to her book on this desk, and with questions on how the mind breaks, and its rhythms and repairs.

It is through Crysta that I first caught a glimpse of a world where the cultural margins were as thin as half alleyways where people and meanings met. Crysta was, in her work and life, inclusive and embracing of people who occupied all the edges of normal. She herself was sometimes on an edge, and she folded it back toward the rest of us in her poems so we could feel its raw tenderness.

Take, for example, these lines from Crysta's poem—

The Sane and the Insane

My thoughts are more exciting
when I'm not on meds.
On medication, I think

of vacuuming the carpet
to get rid of any bugs
Bonnie may have left
when she curled into a fetal position
on the rug last Sunday.

Later, Bonnie's three lit cigarettes in an ashtray stand for themselves, concretely, and for a mind unmoored from its tether of language. We watch with Bonnie, in the same quiet despair, as her cigarettes, as fragments, burn.

Crysta won a Richard Hugo House Award for the quality and humanity of her work. She was an essential part of a place, in a frame of time, that was the Hugo House community then. She sat on the porch and greeted everyone who walked through the doors: whatever the weather, and whatever mood or muse the person wrestled with that day. I always asked her what she was working on: a poem or her poetry manuscript. She answered questions with a half-smile that made her seem to see more than she said or more than the moment seemed to consciously carry.

One morning she handed me a manila envelope. "I thought you might like this," she said. "I read your article about the kid. This will help you."

The article she referenced was something I had written for a newspaper about a young schizophrenic man I had supervised in a homeless employment program. The young man had been confusing and deeply compelling. He had gone in and out of jail several times. I could see how sensitive he was, but I didn't understand the mechanisms of his illness.

Crysta did. The article she handed me that morning was about new perspectives on schizophrenia. It explored the human phenomena—the way Brian Koehler, Marilyn Charles, James Grotstein, or Harold Searles does—and not just the urge to make pathology, of psychosis.

The gift of the envelope was offered a few weeks after the first time Crysta and I had coffee together. It was on a day she was reading poetry magazines and writing in the Hugo House library.

We walked to a nearby café. Crysta seemed more animated when we were out in public. She described her history as a Parks and Recreation employee and then as a journalist in the army. She told me how much she liked to roller skate, and that she lived in a public housing building downtown. She had a boyfriend who lived near her, and a psychologist from the Veteran's Administration who came to all of her readings. She had been diagnosed with cancer a few years back and had undergone treatment. The cancer was in remission, she said.

Crysta's honesty and directness impressed me. She didn't blink much when looking at the world. In the same way, the figure in Crysta's painting, *Green Cammie*, on the cover of her book keeps wide-eyed vigil. The face resembles a Modigliani mask: fragmented into parts, with a face for each eye. One face looks outward, beaking to the side.

In the environment of the painting, animal stripes cross the furniture behind and beneath the seated figure, who wears stylized animal stripes on her military shirt. All the animal prints converge, leaving a primal sense: a fear of what's to come, or the dread of what's gone before, that could not be named. The painting seems to personify the state of dissociation. Bright underwear shows like a foreign flag. Child-sized legs precariously bear up an adult torso. A white shirt behind the central figure has its own ghoulish face, as if a hallucinatory voice took a shape.

There were other paintings Crysta showed me over the years, and ones that I have seen more recently hanging in her friend Deborah Woodard's house. Some of Crysta's other paintings that were lighter in subject and tone remind me of sketches by Joni Mitchell. Photos of the young Crysta also remind me of young Joni Mitchell a bit. Crysta's photos have the same unassuming innocence and a long-ing to connect like a bird in songs layered in rhythms. *Green Cammie* seemed like Crysta's darkest painting.

On another afternoon, when we met for coffee, Crysta brought the latest version of her manuscript. Afterwards, I kept it in my Hugo House office. The poems seemed ordered in a Mobius strip spiral of grief and redemption.

When I left Hugo House to attend school I lost touch with Crysta. She called a few times to see about having coffee. I got caught up in an exploration of soma and psyche until I came to understand that the body/mind question was a riddle, older than Hippocrates. Much brighter minds than mine had been confounded by it.

In the meantime, Crysta had been struggling intimately with what I tried to grab in the abstract. I didn't know that her cancer had returned, and I was surprised to learn about her death in June 2008. A year or so earlier I had come across her manuscript and the schizo-phrenia article again, right before starting an internship at a psychi-atric hospital. I ended up exploring whether music could serve, for people with psychosis, as a kind of language for what was otherwise ineffable.

Crysta came back into my life, through her book of poetry, while I was trying to understand the unconscious communications of Tool and Lady Gaga and Glenn Gould. She helped me, as she already had helped, and again. In retrospect, Crysta always offered steady guidance and a poetic doorway into the more unchartered territories of humanness where she was already at home.

II.

Crysta was really amazing at bridging the sometimes-narrow gulf between madness and sanity. She tuned into subtle and sensitive levels of silence, and how despair or a person's deep sense of expendability could resonate in a gesture. In "Tony's Finger," the narrator kicks his severed body part with its dirt and scars into a ditch. In "Green Cammie," we learn that the narrator has found her favorite army camouflage shirt at a garage sale as evidence of, "The dead remains left to relatives/ who pack up."

Crysta didn't flinch from exploring cultural institutions (the army, the family, the hospital) in which safe containment can get distorted and old versions of perversions can get re-enacted, wearing new faces and well-pressed uniforms. Crysta tried to make sense of the kinds of absurdity that twist impressionable minds: a child showers with her father while an anxious mother waits but does not move to protect her daughter. In another poem, a woman is given pills to help her forget about being sexually used and exploited. Crysta explored the complex ways in which a person unlinks from pain in order to survive.

III.

As a way to honor and to thank Crysta (and to thank Deborah Woodard, too, for stewarding Crysta's poetry into print and performance), I took several *Green Cammie* books to two conferences in late 2010. They were psychological conferences but one of them had a literary bent. That was the conference in Stockbridge, Massachusetts, at Austen Riggs, a psychodynamic treatment center founded in 1919. Riggs is an anomaly within the dominant modern medical model of pills, empirical proofs, and pathologies. At Riggs, patients who haven't done well with other kinds of treatment talk to psychotherapists several times a week. They take arts-based classes; they write; they learn new skills and improve through therapeutic human connections. The conference at Austen Riggs was for the International Society for the Psychological Treatments of the Schizophrenias and other Psychoses (ISPS). People who experience psychosis can belong to ISPS along with physicians, psychologists, social workers, nurses, family members, and advocates. The main speakers at the conference were French sociologists Françoise Davoine and Jean-Max Gaudi lliére, who co-wrote *History Beyond Trauma*. The main premise of the book, and part of the life's work of the authors, is to illustrate how madness is born from trauma, and through generations of unspoken trauma. When the silent histories of war and human cruelty finally emerge, to be uttered and contained (as Crysta did in poems) we can arrive at an expanded sense of health and freedom. I gave Françoise a copy of Crysta's book. I gave another copy to the other speaker, Joanne Greenberg, who wrote *I Never Promised You A Rose Garden*. That book was a fictional account of Greenberg's struggles with schizophrenia and her successful treatment under the care of Frieda Fromm-Reichmann, a gifted psychoanalyst. Greenberg was a phenomenal storyteller, and a great maker of metaphors. She was witty. She took off her shoes to talk. She seemed like someone Crysta would have liked: a straight shooter, with charming eccentricities.

Rain

I took a break,
stood by the fountain
near the cafeteria.
A boy about five
came out to the edge
of the garden
where water dripped
from an overhang
to put his hands
in the rain,
rub them together.
He stuck his tennis shoe out,
leaned his chest,
then shoulder

into the drip,
pulled his sweatshirt
open at the neck, said, "Yikes! That tickles."
Put his hair
under, said, "Yow!
I just got shot in the head."

—Crysta Casey

Crysta's books also traveled with me to a conference on Early Onset Psychosis in Amsterdam. I have no idea why I was invited to present at that conference (there was one other arts-based poster among aisles and aisles of empirical research). One of the main speakers discussed potential changes to the upcoming fifth edition of the *Diagnostic and Statistical Manual of Mental Disorders (DSM-IV*, the psychiatric Bible). There was a big controversy over whether to add in a pre-psychotic diagnosis called Attenuated Psychosis Syndrome, which would allow physicians to preventatively treat young people whom they anticipate might develop psychosis. This is tricky and dangerous territory. (If you're interested in this topic, read the January, 2011, issue of *Wired* magazine.) If I keep with the metaphor of cultural margins here, this new diagnosis would enlarge, not diminish, margins.

In Amsterdam, I gave a copy of Crysta's book to a friend, Csilla, who was writing a commissioned report on various alternative treatments for psychosis. Then I took Crysta's book with me to the Van Gogh Museum. It seemed like a good place to find refuge in the chaos of cross-purposes, and a good place to end this essay, standing in front Van Gogh's painting, *The Mulberry Tree*.

I hope to keep bringing Crysta along to conferences as a muse and as a diplomat of sanity.

May her poems linger with us like smoke and music on the intimacy of all porches. Beaks facing out and our eyes unblinking.

—Trisha Ready

Teaching Crysta Casey:
She lived a hard life well, even wonderfully

I first met Crysta in the early 1990s, before her first collection of poetry, *Heart Clinic,* was published (1993). She came to the basement of the University branch library to read her poems on open mic at the "It's About Time Writers Reading Series," which I was emceeing. She read in a loud, scratchy, almost monotonic voice. All the while she rocked. I began rocking with her. The audience, the room, —the library itself—all seemed to be rocking. We were mesmerized. Crysta could do that to people. She'd grab you and she was yours for life. That is what Crysta did to people—she grabbed them—and it's what her work does; it grabs.

I teach Crysta Casey. I study her. She continues to open doors for me; and as she does, she opens that many more for others. Recently in my women's writing class, "Poeming the Silence," I taught two two-hour segments using Crysta's poem "Inner Feelings." It appears on a broadside next to her painting, "Self-Portrait in Overalls." I presented a broadside to each of the women sitting around my table, and over a two-week period provided the following writing exercises based on it: 1) After reading the poem, free associate: write whatever comes to mind. 2) Study the painting, "Self-Portrait", and write a response. 3) Trace your hands in your notebook and, within the outline, write a letter to Crysta.

By now class participants were familiar with Crysta—through stories I told them of my friendship with her—but, more important, by reading poems from *Heart Clinic* and *Green Cammie.* They learned about the U.S. Marine Corps, the schizophrenia, the burning, and the father she showered with. From *Green Cammie:*

Inner Feelings

George wants me to express
inner feelings. I hear
vague voices above or beyond
the radio. The walls talk.
All week I have been with people.
I am glad to be alone now.
Tonight I washed hair in the shower,
pulled on sweats, cuddly cottons.
Tossed salad with avocado,
tomato and artichoke hearts
for dinner. Now I sip decaffeinated
Irish cream. My coffee carafe
did not crack this morning
the way my thoughts did. Water
pearls on the ceiling
of the shower. I patted bath powder
on my chest and back, a puff
under the elastic of my underwear,
belly and rear. I am clean; my hair dries
in the air. The same Vance Hotel
sign that I saw out the barred window
of the institution shines red
where I now live.
I am lonely for myself. I will read
a story aloud. My voice will break
the silence.
                    —Crysta Casey

The predominant themes that emerged in all three exercises were the light, shadow and dark in Crysta's work. For Joanna Gerber, there is loneliness coupled with a questioning toward resolution, "Maybe the other sounds [which keep her lonely] will keep me together."

Less Lonely for Myself
—after Crysta Casey

I am glad to be alone now,
but am I ever really alone?
The walls talk, people are around.
It always seems they are spinning,
unpredictable.
If I read aloud, will I then
be less lonely for myself?
I don't think I know.
Maybe the other sounds will keep me
together—the voices, the radio, the walls,
decaf coffee, water pouring,
my voice.
                    —Joanna Gerber

But, as Rebecca Crichton's interprets, Crysta's poems do not only help us find the loneliness and vulnerability in ourselves; they also help to uncover our strengths and beauty. In her prose piece, "Make yourself comfortable," Rebecca remembers that she is capable of creating comfort for others, and she realizes that she knows how to get it for herself when she allows. Rebecca reminds us that, "Nurturing comes from warm liquid or creamy purees or piquant flavors... ":

77

"The happiest meals have many choices and textures, mix and match ingredients. Spiky tapenade and soft goat cheese, crisp crackers, crunchy pickles, silky hummus—the Mediterranean palate always a pleasure with sun held in the flavors, reminders of ancient habits and places."

Crysta's "sweats and cuddly cottons" remind Rebecca that:

"Soft shawls and hugging scarves always subdue the slight shiver. I am often one step away from wanting to be cuddled in warmth. My bed has layers of pillows that back me as I settle with the books I am reading. I feel most safe, most certain of my own ability to care for myself, when robed in fleece, a book propped on my chest."

Crysta's work is open and accessible enough to allow readers to project themselves into what they read. For Nikki Nordstrom, Crysta seems worried, concerned about what she needs to get done. In "Revelation of I," Nikki writes:

"... What needs to be done ... need not be a conclusion, or even a period. Just that clear sparkling revelation of I, as it steps back from voices real or imagined, the purification of washing away the debris of contact, the I whose tongue caresses the sensuously smooth side of the avocado, the I of the female who is released by the feel of clean hair."

Karen Baker combined the exercises to write a letter to Crysta with her response to "Self-Portrait in Overalls." In "Dear Crysta," she sees the triumphant YES in Crysta's psyche, in her life and thought:

Dear Crysta

*Your wistful look up to the corner
of the mirror
gives me pause.*

78

Did you see the shadow there,
the one behind the dresser, spreading dark wings,
a threat among the roses on the wallpaper?

Did you see your face asymmetric with shadow and light?
Did a camera catch you looking like this, your
perspective off, feeling deeply the pain of your aloneness?

Life belongs to the ones
who say yes.
No matter how many
shadows cross their face.

Life belongs to the ones with the courage
to put pen to paper,
to put paint on canvas.
Life belongs to the ones
who can stare down the cameras
and the mirrors
and the shadows.
　　　　　　　—Karen Baker

Pat Gunn's work reflects her own as well as Crysta's confusion in the physicality of the material world but, in the end, for both, the esoteric is most meaningful:

On Casey's Self-Portrait in Overalls

The perspective's all wrong.
Your elbow is too close
to the desk leg. The viewer's
eye can't find focus.

79

Your left arm is several
inches shorter than your right.
The asymmetry is hard
on the eye.

Beyond your face
you paint a window,
a curtain, a lamp, a clock
a mug festooned with
pencils.
The eye does not
know where to look.

It's a funny thing
*   your art*
Too close, too far,
too cluttered.

The eye does not know
where to look.
*   But the heart*
The heart sees intimately.
—Pat Gunn

I told the class the story about the famous poet who told
Crysta she was not a poet, that her words did not form poems. They
were not poetry. To this Karen responded:

Dear Crysta,

To that man,
the one who said you

80

weren't a poet,
I say, Michael Jordan was
cut from his high school
basketball team.
What would success look like
without some failure to light
the way.

Words march across
the page like ants.
Small soldiers
making the way.

Victory is believing in yourself.
Victory is marching on
breaking down the voices
the ones who say "No, you can't,"
"shouldn't,
must not,
will never."

Victory is putting your face to the sun and shining.
Looking at the world with fresh eyes.
Victory is taking joy in red flowers,
in coffee
in being home.
—Karen Baker

Teaching Crysta Casey—reading and studying her work
—provides me with experience that I am still uncovering. For me,
Crysta's work is the best of poetry. It is alive and whole, it reflects
the human condition in all its convolutions and ambivalences—the
rhyme and song of life alongside the terror.

Nikki: *"What was stunning to me was Crysta's poetic ability, in spite of the degree of her illness. As we were reading Crysta's work in class it was difficult for me to imagine how she had accomplished so much while in the throes of such a disabling disease."*

Pat Gunn's response to our drawing exercise sums it up well:

Dear Crysta,

These hands held fingers wide,
cover a face, a heart, a head.
These hands held fingers wide,
cover an ear, an eye, a limb.
     That's the deception
     of the corporal world.
These hands can't shield
your wounds.
This paper, ephemeral and pulpy,
This is your salve.
     —Pat Gunn

Participants in my "Poeming the Silence" class clearly demonstrate that while Crysta Casey's poems document the specificity of her own life, they also provide insight into all of our lives. Thank you, Crysta. I miss you.

—Esther Altshul Helfgott

—**Esther Altshul Helfgott** is the author of *Listening to Mozart: Poems of Alzheimer's* (Yakima, WA.: Cave Moon Press, 2014), *Dear Alzheimer's: A Caregiver's Diary & Poems* (Yakima, WA.: Cave Moon Press, 2013) and *The Homeless One: A Poem in Many Voices* (Seattle: Kota Press, 2000). Essays and poems appear in American Imago: Psychoanalysis and the Human Sciences, HistoryLink, Journal of Poetry Therapy, Maggid: A Journal of Jewish Literature and most recently in Eric Pfeiffer, M.D.'s *Caregiving in Alzheimer's and Other Dementias* (New Haven & London: Yale University Press, 2015) and Gary Glazner's *Dementia Arts: Celebrating Creativity in Elder Care*, (Health Professions Press, 2014). She has a Ph.D in history from the University of Washington and is at work on a biography of the Viennese-born Seattle psychoanalyst, Dr. Edith Buxbaum.

—**Trisha Ready** is a writer and a clinical psychologist, who had the good fortune to work at Hugo House until 2005. She has had essays and articles published in a number of venues including *The Stranger, Longreads, Music and Medicine,* and *Psychoanalysis, Culture, and Society.* She has a forthcoming book entitled *Music in Therapeutic Practice: Using Rhythm to Bridge Communication Barriers* from Rowman & Littlefield.

Acknowledgements

The Estate of Crysta E. Casey thanks the editors of the following journals in which these poems appeared, sometimes in slightly different form:

Bellowing Ark: "Adam and Eve," "Flying," "Rude Awakening in the Public Affairs Office," "Self-Portrait," "Resident Poet"
Convolvulus: "A Curse, for Captain Bowman"
Fine Madness: "Rain"
Nobody's Orphan Child: "Green Cammie"
ONTHEBUS: "Taking Meds On Time"
Pontoon: "Hell and Heaven," "San Luis Rey Officers' Club," "The Sane and The Insane"
Real Change: "Two Mirrors At The Bus Stop Near The Hurricane Café"
The Licton Springs Review: "Divertimento No. 2 in D, K. 131, Mozart"
Vietnam Veterans Against the War: "Poem for an Unknown Soldier"

"Rain" also appeared in *March Hares, The Best Poems from Fine Madness, 1982-2002, Fine Madness*, 2002.

"Visiting Mother" and "Shifting" first appeared in *Heart Clinic* (Bellowing Ark Press, 1993).

A number of these poems appeared in the chapbook, *Green Cammie* (Floating Bridge, 2010).

"Crysta Casey" by Trisha Ready and "Teaching Crysta Casey: She Lived a Hard Life Well, Even Wonderfully" by Esther Altshul Helfgott first appeared in *Raven Chronicles, Vol. 16, No. 1-2, Matters of the Spirit*, 2011-2012.

We extend our thanks to Crysta Casey's friends in the literary and veteran communities, and to the Seattle Veterans Health Care System, which worked so hard on Crysta's behalf. We are especially grateful to Floating Bridge Press and Cave Moon Press, the publishers of Crysta's posthumous collections, *Green Cammie* and *Rules for Walking Out*. Knowing that these books are published and available would have delighted Crysta.

—Esther Altshul Helfgott, George Saronto Stamas, and Deborah Woodard, acting on behalf of the Estate of Crysta E. Casey

A tip of the hat to Elizabeth Austen, Lana Hechtman Ayers, Anna Balint, Phoebe Bosche, Anita K. Boyle, Rebecca Brown, Mitch Cohen, Christine Deavel, Chris Dusterhoff, Kathleen Flenniken, the late Paula Jones Gardiner, John Gorski, Mike Hickey, Kayt Hoch, Holly Hughes, Nancy Kennedy, Irene Leyson, Doug Johnson, J.W. Marshall, Gerry McFarland, Brian McGuigan, Dr. Marcus Nemuth, Kathleen Notley, Arne Pihl, Chris Storey, and Trisha Ready.

Also by Crysta Casey

Heart Clinic 1993
Green Cammie 2010

eBooks

Celebration 2013
Yesterday My Name Was Wine Bottle 2014

About the Author

Crysta Casey (1952-2008) was born in Pasadena, California. She graduated from The State University of New York, Stony Brook, in 1976, where she was one of the founding members of The Women Writers Workshop. After college, she became the first woman hired by the City of Irvine, California, in Parks and Maintenance. In 1978, she enlisted in the all-new voluntary military, serving in the U.S. Marine Corps as a journalist, then as a self-declared "Resident Poet" until her honorable discharge under medical conditions in 1980. She moved to Seattle, Washington in the early 1980s, where she studied with the poet Nelson Bentley and collaborated with Esther Altshul Helfgott on the It's About Time Writers Reading Series. Her first collection of poetry, *Heart Clinic*, was published in 1993 (Bellowing Ark Press). In 2004 she received a Hugo House Award from Richard Hugo House, and, in 2006, she was a finalist for Seattle Poet Populist. In 2010, Floating Bridge Press brought out a chapbook of her work, *Green Cammie*. *Rules for Walking Out* was the last manuscript Crysta completed and approved before her death at the Seattle VA in the spring of 2008. Crysta's papers are housed in the University of Washington Libraries, Special Collections. The photograph of Crysta and her beloved cat Varmint, included below, was taken in her Belltown apartment, in downtown Seattle.